DATE DUE

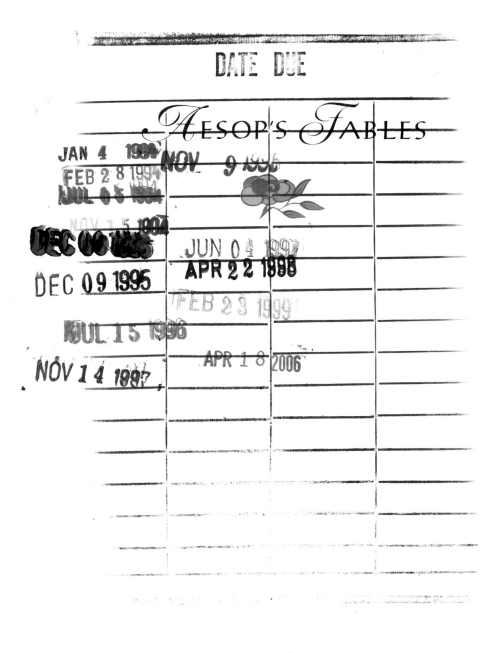

Aesop's Fables

Aesop's Fables

ILLUSTRATED BY
Safaya Salter

Retold by Anne Gatti

Gulliver Books
Harcourt Brace Jovanovich, Publishers
San Diego   New York   London

HBJ

Text copyright © 1992 by Pavilion Books, Ltd.
Illustrations copyright © 1992 by Safaya Salter

First published 1992 by Pavilion Books
First U.S. edition 1992

Requests for permission to make copies of any part
of the work should be mailed to: Permissions Department,
Harcourt Brace Jovanovich, Publishers, 8th Floor,
Orlando, Florida 32887.

Library of Congress Cataloging-in-Publication Data
Aesop's fables. English. Selections.
Aesop's fables/illustrated by Safaya Salter. — 1st U.S. ed.
p.   cm.
"Gulliver books."
Summary: A newly illustrated edition of fifty-eight of Aesop's tales,
complete with the moral for each.
ISBN 0-15-200350-9
1. Fables [1. Fables.] I. Aesop. II. Salter, Safaya, ill.
III. Title.
PZ8.2.A254   1992
398.2′452 — dc20   91-24143

Printed in Spain

A B C D E

for Ameria

TABLE OF CONTENTS

THE BEETLE'S REVENGE

Once there was a hare who was being chased by an eagle. He was almost completely exhausted and very much in need of help. The only creature he could see nearby was a beetle, so he begged the little insect to help him. The beetle told him not to worry, she would protect him. When the eagle swooped down, the beetle called out to her and begged her to leave the poor hare alone. But the mighty eagle, scornful of such a tiny creature, tore the hare to pieces right before the beetle's eyes.

The beetle was furious and promised herself that she would pay the eagle back for ignoring her plea. She watched the eagle closely to find out where the eagle made her nests, and every time the eagle laid some eggs, the beetle flew up and tipped them out so that they broke. The eagle tried and tried to find a nesting site that was out of the beetle's reach but she could not.

Eventually the eagle went to Zeus and begged him to give her, his own sacred bird, a safe place to hatch her chicks. Zeus considered her request and decided to allow her to lay her eggs in his lap. But the beetle saw this. She made a ball of dung, flew high above where Zeus was sitting, and dropped the ball straight into his lap. Without stopping to think, Zeus got up to shake it off and tipped out all the eggs.

MORAL

Don't be fooled by size. A small person can be just as clever as a big person.

The Too-Fat Fox

One afternoon a half-starved fox spotted some meat that had been left by shepherds in the hollow of an oak tree. The fox crept inside the tree and ate and ate. When he had finished, the fox was ready to be on his way, but he found that his stomach had swollen and he could not get out of the tree.

Another fox, who was passing by, heard his cries for help and came up to find out what was the matter. "Well," said the second fox, "I suggest you stay there until you're thin again. Then you'll get out quite easily."

M O R A L

Time solves many problems.

The Lion and the Lost Meal

One evening a lion found a hare asleep. He was very pleased and was just about to eat the hare when he saw a deer running by. Forgetting the hare, he jumped up and chased after the deer, making so much noise that the hare woke up and ran away.

After a long chase the lion realized that he could not catch the deer. Remembering the hare, he returned to where it had been, only to find that, like the deer, it had escaped.

"Serves me right," said the lion, "for leaving the food that I had under my nose in the hope of getting something bigger."

MORAL

Be happy with what you've got.

The Cautious Fox

Once there was a lion who had become too old and weak to hunt for his food. He decided to find another way of feeding himself. He lay down in a cave, pretending to be ill, and whenever any animals came to visit him, he ate them.

One day a fox who had been watching the lion's trick came and stood outside the cave and inquired after the lion's health.

"I'm not at all well," called out the lion. "Why don't you come in and see me?"

"I'd like to," answered the fox, "but I see many tracks going into your cave and none coming out."

MORAL

It is wise to stop at a sign of danger.

BIG AND LITTLE FISH

One evening a fisherman cast his net into the sea. There were many fish in the sea, large and small, and the net was filled immediately. But as the fisherman pulled the net in, the smaller fish escaped through the mesh. The bigger fish also tried to escape, but they could not, and the fisherman ate them.

MORAL

The bigger and more important you are, the easier it is to trap you.

THE LION AND THE ELEPHANT

According to one of the ancient myths of Greece, the great god Prometheus created all the animals, including the magnificent lion. The lion was large and handsome, with razor-sharp teeth and claws. But although he had greater strength than any of the other animals, he complained that Prometheus had made him afraid of cockerels.

"Don't blame me," said Prometheus. "I gave you everything I possibly could. It's your own fault that you're afraid of cockerels."

This only made the lion more upset, and he worried and worried about being a coward. He became so miserable that he wanted to die. Then one day he met an elephant, and the two animals started to talk. While they were chatting, the lion noticed that the elephant kept flapping his enormous ears.

"What's the matter?" he asked. "Can't you keep your ears still?"

Just then a gnat flew around the elephant's head. "Do you see that tiny buzzing creature?" the elephant said, flapping his ears again furiously. "If that wretched thing gets into my ear, I'm sure I'll go mad."

The lion looked at the elephant's anxious expression and thought to himself, "Well, perhaps things aren't as bad as I thought. I may be afraid of cockerels, but I'm not afraid of something as small as that gnat."

MORAL

When you see another person's troubles, your own don't seem so bad.

17

How the Tortoise Got Its Shell

Long ago Zeus invited all the animals to a feast. Everyone came but the tortoise. When Zeus asked him why he stayed away, the tortoise replied, "I like my home." Zeus was so annoyed by this that he made the tortoise carry his home forever after.

MORAL

Don't make excuses for what you know to be laziness.

The Hidden Treasure

An old farmer, who wanted his sons to be successful farmers when he was gone, called them to his side as he lay dying. "My boys," he said, "I'm about to leave this world. I've hidden something in the vineyard, and I want you to search for it when I'm gone. If you do, you'll find everything I have to give you."

The sons thought that their father meant he had hidden some sort of treasure, and after he died, they took out their spades and dug up every inch of soil in the vineyard. The brothers never found any treasure, but because they had dug the soil around the vines so thoroughly, they were rewarded in the summer with a beautiful and plentiful crop of grapes.

MORAL

The fruits of hard work are the best treasure of all.

The Noisy Frog

A lioness was lazing in the sun one day, when she was startled by a loud noise. "What a large animal that must be," she thought. The noise continued and the lioness grew restless. Finally she could stand it no longer. She followed the sound to the edge of a pond. There, behind a large leaf, she found a small frog croaking. "All that worry," she said angrily, "and it was only you." And she crushed the frog with her paw.

MORAL

Too much talk can lead to trouble.

A Lesson in Strength

Once there was a farmer whose sons were always quarreling. The farmer tried to persuade them to stop, but no matter what he said, they continued to argue. So he decided to show them what he meant.

The farmer made his sons bring him a bundle of sticks. He handed the bundle to his oldest son and told him to break it. His son tried but failed. The other sons also tried and failed. Then the farmer untied the bundle and handed his sons the sticks one by one. This time they broke them easily.

"It's the same with you, children," the farmer said. "Together you make a strong team; alone you're easily broken."

MORAL

Unity brings strength; division brings only weakness.

THE CAGED BIRD

There was once a bird in a cage who had a very beautiful voice but who would sing only at night. A bat who was passing by heard her and asked her why she never sang during the day.

"I used to sing in the daytime," she replied sadly, "but then I was captured. Now I've learned my lesson — it's too dangerous to sing during the day. That's why I sing only at night."

"It's a bit late to be careful now," said the bat. "You should have thought about these things before you were caught."

MORAL

Learn to do what is right before you are caught in the wrong; afterward may be too late.

THE FOOLISH MICE

One day a snake and a weasel who shared a house and who usually hunted mice together got into a fight. The mice saw what was happening and scurried boldly out of their holes in search of food, believing that they were safe. But as soon as the snake and the weasel spotted the mice, they stopped fighting and together chased them home.

MORAL

*When your enemies squabble with one another, it
doesn't mean that you are safe.*

THE LION'S SHARE

A lion, a fox, and a wild ass went hunting together, the lion using his strength, the fox his cunning, and the ass his speed. When they had caught a number of animals, the lion divided the catch into three parts.

"I'll take the first part," he said, "because, as king, I hold the highest position in the animal kingdom. And since I'm your equal partner in hunting, I'll take the second part too. As for the third portion, I want that as well, so go away before I gobble you up."

MORAL

Choose your partners carefully.

THE FROGS ASK FOR A KING

The frogs were living happily in a marshy pond, but some of them thought that they needed a king. These frogs sent a petition to Zeus asking if he could appoint a ruler for them. Zeus was amused by the request and dropped a log into their pond crying, "Here is your king!" All the frogs leapt out of the pond, frightened by the splash the log made. After a few minutes, when they saw that the log did not move, they crept cautiously back into the pond to investigate. Still the log didn't move. The frogs who had wanted a king were disappointed and sent another petition to Zeus. "This log is not a very strong king," they complained. "Can't you send us a better ruler?" Now this made Zeus angry. "You don't deserve a better ruler!" he roared. In his anger, he sent as king a water snake whose only interest was to eat as many of the frogs as it could catch. As a result, the frogs were forced to run away to live in another pond.

MORAL

It is better to have a harmless ruler than a tyrant.

THE CLEVER DOG

A dog was lying asleep in a farmyard when suddenly he was attacked by a wolf. The wolf was about to devour him when the dog shouted, "Don't eat me just yet. I'm very scraggly at the moment. But my master is off at a wedding. When he comes back, he'll bring me lots of delicious tidbits. Then I'll make a better meal for you." After thinking it over, the wolf agreed to postpone his meal and went away.

Later the wolf returned to the farm. But the dog was no longer lying in the yard. Instead the wolf saw the dog asleep high up on a roof and called out to him to come down and keep his promise. But the dog replied, "You're too late. Thanks to you I shall always sleep out of harm's way. If you ever find me sleeping on the ground again, I shall deserve to be eaten!"

MORAL

It is wise to learn from your mistakes.

THE JACKDAW WHO CHEATED

Zeus decided that the birds should have a leader, so he announced that the most handsome bird would be king, and he set a day when they should all parade before him.

Although he was very plain, the jackdaw was determined to be king. When all the other birds gathered to preen themselves, the jackdaw stealthily gathered up the feathers that they dropped and fastened them to his own. When the parade began, the jackdaw strutted out onto the sand. Dressed in his colorful plumage he impressed Zeus greatly. But just as Zeus was about to name him king, the other birds realized what had happened. Angrily they plucked at the jackdaw, taking back their feathers until he was just a plain jackdaw again. Then Zeus, angry at having been deceived, chose another bird to be king.

MORAL

Dressing up in borrowed finery does not change who you really are.

Two of a Kind

A man bought an ass from a farmer and took it home. There the new ass went to stand by the laziest of all the asses. Right away the man took the new ass back. "How can you complain?" asked the farmer. "You've only had the ass one day."

"I don't need more time to judge this ass," said the man. "I can tell what it's like by the companion it chose."

MORAL

You will often be judged by the company you keep.

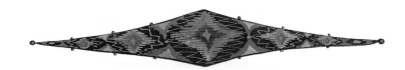

Something Out of Nothing

One day Heracles came across a small apple, which lay on the path where he was walking. Instead of stepping over it, he kicked it, but it didn't roll away. To his astonishment, it doubled in size. Heracles then kicked the apple again, and again it doubled in size. Angrily Heracles kicked it for a third time, and it grew so big that it blocked the path. As he stood staring at it in confusion, Athena appeared before him. "This apple is the spirit of strife and discontent," she explained. "If you provoke it, it will simply grow bigger."

MORAL

Anger only makes a problem worse.

The Shepherd and the Sea

One day a shepherd looked out at the sea. From a distance it looked calm and welcoming, so the shepherd decided to sell his sheep and make a voyage as a trader. But all did not go well. A violent storm nearly destroyed his ship, and although the shepherd made it safely back to land, he lost his cargo. With nothing to sell, he had to go back to tending sheep.

Years later, a passerby remarked on the stillness of the sea. "Don't be fooled," said the shepherd. "The sea has many moods."

MORAL

Appearances are sometimes deceptive.

The Selfish Horse

A man set off on a journey with many baskets, taking both his horse and his donkey to carry the load. But after many miles the little donkey could no longer carry all his burden. He begged the horse to help him, but the horse was quite comfortable as he was and refused. Soon the exhausted donkey could walk no further, and he collapsed in the road. The man, who had no intention of stopping, put all the donkey's baskets on the horse's back and continued on his way. "I wish I had helped the donkey earlier," wailed the horse. "Now I have to carry the whole burden alone."

MORAL

It is better to share burdens.

The Fox and the Stork

Some time ago a stork, who had just arrived from another country, was invited to dinner by a fox. The stork was delighted to be asked and went to the fox's home, feeling good and hungry. When she got there, she found that the fox had prepared some clear soup, which he served in dishes that were so shallow that she could only wet her long beak. She could do nothing but watch her host lap up his supper, and when he had finished, she went home still hungry.

Not long after this the stork invited the fox to dine with her. The fox accepted the invitation, but when he arrived he found that she had prepared a thick soup, which she served in tall jars. She stuck her beak down into her jar and enjoyed her meal while the fox, almost fainting with hunger and unable to reach his food, could only stand and watch.

When the stork had finished, she smiled at the fox. "I'm only following your example," she said.

MORAL

Treat others as you like to be treated yourself.

34

THE GRATEFUL EAGLE

One day a small boy found a magnificent eagle caught in a trap. He thought that the bird was too beautiful to live in captivity, so he undid the trap and let the bird go free.

Some days later the eagle saw the boy sitting by an old wall at the edge of a field. The bird flew down and snatched the boy's headband off his head. The boy jumped up and chased the bird, who soon dropped the headband on the ground and flew away. As the boy picked up his headband and turned to make his way back to the wall, he felt quite angry.

But when he reached the edge of the field, he discovered that the wall had collapsed right where he had been sitting, and he realized that the eagle had repaid him for his own earlier kindness.

M O R A L

One good deed often follows another.

THE PROUD FIR TREE

One day a fir tree and a thorn bush were arguing. The thorn bush was angry because the fir was singing its own praises. "I am tall and handsome and will be used for building such important things as church roofs and ships."

"But think of the sharp axes and saws that will cut you," replied the thorn bush. "Then you'll wish you were more like me."

MORAL

Do not be proud of your beauty; it may be your downfall.

THE PARROT AND THE CAT

Some time ago a man bought a parrot and took her home. The man allowed his new parrot to fly all around the house, and the parrot settled in very quickly. One day soon after she arrived, the house cat came across the parrot perched on the mantelpiece, chattering away quite happily to herself. The cat, who had not yet met the parrot, was most put out, and asked, in a rather frosty voice, who she was and where she had come from. The parrot replied that the master had just bought her.

"Well," said the cat, "you do have a nerve. Imagine a newcomer like you making such a racket, when I, who was born in this house, am not allowed even to meow. If I do, my master gets furious and chases me away."

"Well," replied the parrot, "my advice to you is to leave this house and find yourself a new home. You see, the master of the house doesn't mind my voice, but I'm afraid it seems he doesn't like yours."

MORAL

*It is better to find people who like you than to stay
among those who don't.*

The Dog in the Manger

One day an ill-tempered dog was sniffing around a manger full of barley. The dog didn't like barley and was about to leave when a hungry zebra came by. Suddenly the dog decided not to leave; instead he barked fiercely and threatened the zebra.

M O R A L

The greatest selfishness is to stop others having what you yourself cannot enjoy.

The Wise Martin

When mistletoe first started to grow on oak trees, people found that they could use its glue to trap birds. A martin soon realized how dangerous this plant was. She called all the birds together and advised them to tear it off the trees.

But the other birds just made fun of the martin. They said that she didn't know what she was talking about, so the martin gave up trying to warn them. Instead she asked the people if she could live with them. The people, who admired her cleverness, welcomed her. Soon she was nesting safely in one of their houses. But the other birds were caught in traps made of mistletoe glue.

MORAL

Be prudent and you will live a long life.

The Man and His Wig

One day a mischievous gust of wind lifted a man's wig from his head and blew it away. The passersby laughed at the man, but he replied with a smile, "It's not surprising that I can't keep my hair on, because it doesn't grow there — and the man on whose head it first grew couldn't keep it on his head, either."

M O R A L

Never be ashamed of something that you do not bring upon yourself.

The Cat Who Fell in Love

Once there was a cat who fell in love with a handsome man and begged Aphrodite to change her into a human being. The goddess felt sorry for the cat and agreed, provided the cat would give up all her feline ways. The cat, who was very eager, promised she would, and so Aphrodite transformed her into an enchanting girl. When the man saw the girl, he was so struck by her beauty that he married her immediately.

Some days later the newlyweds were sitting at their fireside when a mouse ran by. Without thinking, the girl jumped up and pounced on the mouse. Too late, she remembered her promise. Sadly, Aphrodite changed her back into a cat.

M O R A L

Changing your looks will not turn you into a different person.

42

The Amaranth and the Rose

An amaranth said to the rose that grew beside it, "How lovely you are. It's no wonder that gods and humans are so enchanted by you. Not only are you the most perfectly shaped flower but you have an exquisite perfume as well."

"Thank you for the compliments," said the rose, "but remember, I live only a short while, and even if no one cuts me, I wither quickly. You, however, continue to bloom and always stay as fresh as you are now."

MORAL

It is better to be happy with little and live long than to live a short life filled with empty luxuries.

The Boastful Hunter

Once, while looking for a lion's tracks, a hunter met a forester. The hunter, who was very pleased with himself, told the forester that he wanted to trap a lion and asked the forester if he had seen the lion's tracks or if he knew where the lion's lair was. The forester replied that, better still, he could show the hunter the lion itself. At this the hunter turned very pale, and his teeth began to chatter.

"It's a-a-a-ll right," he stammered, "I'm only l-l-l-looking for its trail."

MORAL

Courage is proven by deeds, not by words alone.

THE SELFISH BEES

Long ago the bees decided that they wanted to keep all their honey for themselves. So they went to Zeus and asked him to give them the power to sting anyone who dared to come near their honeycombs.

Zeus granted their request, but he was angry with the selfish bees. As a punishment he ordered that not only should they lose their stings if they used them but that they should also lose their lives.

MORAL

Selfishness brings its own punishment.

THE JEALOUS CAMEL

One night a monkey got up in front of a gathering of animals and began to dance. His audience clapped so loudly and paid him so many compliments that a camel standing in the crowd grew jealous. Thinking that he could get just as much attention, the camel went out in front of the crowd and tried to dance like the monkey.

But the clumsy camel couldn't dance well, and he looked so silly as he shuffled around that the crowd booed him and sent him away.

MORAL

Don't try to be something that you're not.

THE LIONESS AND THE VIXEN

One day a vixen passed a lioness in her den. "You're not as mighty as you think," said the vixen. "You never manage to give birth to more than one cub at a time."

"True," the lioness quietly replied, "but that one cub is always a lion."

MORAL

It's quality, not quantity, that counts.

THE EXILED JACKDAW

Once there was a large jackdaw who despised the other mem-
bers of his flock because they were all smaller than he was. He
left his flock and went looking for a flock of crows, hoping he
could live with them instead. But the jackdaw looked and
sounded unfamiliar to the crows, and they turned on him and
drove him away.

The disappointed jackdaw returned to his own flock. But
the other jackdaws, who were angry at the way he had insulted
them, wouldn't allow him back, and so the foolish jackdaw had
to live alone.

MORAL

Don't expect those you have insulted
to welcome you back.

THE WISE CICADA

For a long time a cicada sat chirping in a tree while a hungry fox sat below, thinking up a plan to catch and eat her. Finally the fox looked up at the cicada and spoke to her, showering her with compliments about her musical voice. Then he suggested that the cicada should come down so that he could see how beautiful she was.

The cicada, however, was too clever to fall into the fox's trap. Instead she broke a leaf off the tree and dropped it. Thinking it was the cicada herself, the fox dashed forward to catch it. Too late, he realized he had been tricked.

"I knew you were hoping to eat me," said the cicada. "You see, I've been on my guard against foxes ever since the day I saw cicadas' wings in a fox's droppings."

MORAL

Wise people learn from their neighbors' mistakes.

The Fox and the Mask

A curious fox once crept into an actor's house and rummaged through all his things to see what he could find. In a trunk of costumes he came across a wonderful mask shaped like a hobgoblin's head, which had been made by a talented artist. The fox held it up in his paws to admire it and said, "What a magnificent head! It's a pity it has no brain."

MORAL

Good looks are not always
accompanied by a good brain.

THE SHIPWRECK

A rich man was on a voyage across the sea when a terrible storm blew up. The rich man's ship capsized, and everyone was thrown into the sea. All the passengers then began to swim for their lives, except the rich man, who raised his arms to heaven and called to the goddess Athena, offering her all kinds of riches if she would save him. The other passengers soon reached pieces of wreckage and, clinging to them, shouted back to the praying man: "Don't leave it all to the goddess; you must swim, too."

MORAL

The gods help those who help themselves.

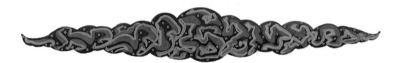

THE TWO THIEVES

One day when a wolf had stolen a sheep from the flock and was carrying it off to his lair, a lion sprang out at him from behind a bush. The wolf dropped the sheep and retreated. The lion picked up the sheep and started to carry it away. "But you can't take it!" cried the wolf indignantly. "That's *my* sheep." The lion only laughed.

"No, it isn't," he replied. "It belongs to the shepherd, and you stole it. And now I'm stealing it from you."

MORAL

One thief is as bad as another.

A Lesson in Humility

A vain man once read to Aesop some dull essays he had written about himself and asked the wise Aesop, "Do you think I'm too boastful?" Aesop replied, "You are right to praise yourself, for no one else ever will."

The boastful usually have little to boast about.

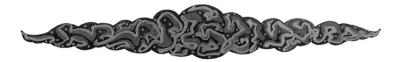

The Dishonest Doctor

An elderly woman, who lived in a house full of beautiful paintings and ornaments, asked a doctor to treat her bad eyes. The doctor came, put ointment on her eyelids, and told her to keep her eyes closed for a while. Then, as she sat there, he stole one or two of her valuable possessions. Each time he visited, he took another item, until the old woman's house was almost bare. One day he arrived to treat her, but he found two policemen waiting to arrest him. "I'm not a thief!" he protested. "I didn't say you were a thief," said the old lady, slyly, "but you are a bad doctor. Before you treated my eyes, I could see all my belongings. Now I can't see any of them."

A thief will always be caught.

THE GREEDY DOG

A dog was crossing a river with a piece of meat in his mouth when, looking down, he saw his reflection in the water. Thinking the reflection was another dog carrying another piece of meat in its mouth, the dog dropped his meat and made a grab for the other dog's piece. But, of course, he ended up with nothing. His own piece fell into the water and was swept away by the river, and the other piece disappeared with it.

MORAL

Greedy people end up with less.

The Tortoise and the Hare

A tortoise and a hare once got into an argument about who could run faster. They decided that the best way to settle the matter was to have a race, so they fixed a time and a place to meet and then went their separate ways.

The hare was so confident that he was going to win that he didn't bother to start at the agreed time. Instead he decided to take a nap. He told himself that when he woke, he could easily overtake the tortoise and win the race.

The tortoise, however, set off on time. He plodded along, going slowly, but not stopping for a single rest. On and on he went. Eventually, just as the hare was waking up, the tortoise crossed the finish line. The tortoise had won the race.

MORAL

Slow and steady wins the race.

THE GREEDY ANT

Once there was a farmer who was unhappy with what he had and kept stealing his neighbors' crops. His greed made Zeus so angry that he decided to change him into the tiny insect that we now call the ant. But even when the farmer's body was changed, his character remained the same. He and all his kind still go to and fro, collecting other people's wheat and barley and storing it up for themselves.

MORAL

Once a thief, always a thief.

THE BEAR'S MESSAGE

Two friends were traveling together through a forest when suddenly a bear appeared. One of the friends scrambled up the nearest tree and hid among the branches. The other, realizing that the bear would catch up with him at any moment, threw himself down on the ground and pretended to be dead.

The bear came up to investigate and sniffed the man all over. The man was scared, but he lay still and held his breath, for he had been told that a bear will not bother a corpse.

Eventually the bear lost interest and ambled off. The man who had scrambled up the tree climbed down and asked his friend what the bear had whispered in his ear.

"He told me," the second man replied, "that in the future I should travel with people who stand by their friends when there's danger."

MORAL

True friends stay together, even through the bad times.

The Proud Cockerel

Once there were two cockerels who fought on and on for the attention of the hens in their barnyard. Finally one was defeated, and he ran away to hide in a dark corner. His proud rival climbed onto a high wall and crowed and crowed.

Just then an eagle swooped down, grabbed the noisy cockerel in his talons, and carried it off. The other cockerel, safely out of view in his hiding place, waited until the eagle had gone. Then he came out and continued wooing the hens.

MORAL

Pride comes before a fall.

The Ant and the Dove

A thirsty ant crawled down to the edge of a stream for a drink, but just at that moment the current swelled and the ant was carried away. A dove who was flying by saw the ant, broke off a twig, and threw it into the water. The ant crawled onto the twig and in a moment was washed safely onto dry land.

Later that day a hunter appeared with some sticks smeared with lime and started to set them in position to catch the dove. When the ant saw this, she bit the man sharply on the foot. With a shriek of pain, the hunter dropped the sticks and clutched his foot. The dove, frightened by the noise, flew off.

MORAL

One good turn deserves another.

The Bald Man

A man whose hair was going gray had two wives, one young and the other old. The young wife was embarrassed about having an old man as her husband, and when he was with her, she pulled out as many of his gray hairs as she could. The old wife, on the other hand, liked the man to look as old as she herself was, and she pulled out his black hairs. As a result, the poor man was soon completely bald.

MORAL

You can't please everyone all the time.

Jumping to Conclusions

A lion and a man were walking along a path together when they came across a large stone at the side of the road. On the stone was carved a picture of a hunter pinning a frightened lion to the ground. The man pointed to the carving and joked, "There's proof that men are stronger than lions." But the lion smiled. "Not at all," he replied. "If lions could carve, you would find many pictures of men being eaten."

MORAL

Don't jump to conclusions.

True Friends

A great man once had a small house built for himself to live in. A passerby remarked that it was rather small for such a man. "Why don't you build a grander house for all your visitors?" she asked. "This house is large enough to hold all my true friends," replied the man.

MORAL

True friends are few and far between.

The Stomach and the Feet

The stomach and the feet were arguing about who was stronger. The feet insisted that they were far stronger than the stomach because they carried it about all the time.

"That's true," replied the stomach, "but if I stopped providing you with nourishment, you wouldn't be able to carry me or move yourselves."

MORAL

People depend on one another more than they realize.

THE REED AND THE OLIVE TREE

One day an olive tree began arguing with a reed about who was stronger and could better survive the force of the wind and rain. The olive tree accused the reed of being weak and criticized it for being easily bent by even the tiniest puff of wind. The reed didn't say a word.

A few days later there was a terrible storm. The wind raged. The reed let itself be tossed around and bent by the gusts, and it survived the storm without any damage. The proud olive tree, on the other hand, tried to prove its strength by standing up to the wind and was broken in two as a result.

MORAL

Sometimes it is better to bend with the wind than to stand against it.

When a Man Means Business

One year a pair of larks made their nest in a field of unripe corn. They fed their chicks on the green shoots until the chicks had grown their feathers and were ready to fly. Around this time the farmer inspected his field and saw that the corn was ripe.

"Perhaps I should ask all my friends to help me with the harvesting," he said.

One of the chicks overheard him and told its father. "It's time for us to find another home," said the chick.

"We don't need to move for a while," replied the father. "The person who relies on his friends to do a job for him is not too bothered about getting it·done."

A few days later the farmer visited the field again and saw the ears of corn dropping off in the heat of the sun.

"Tomorrow I must hire some men to harvest this corn and tie it up in sheaves," he said.

"*Now* we had better move on," said the lark to his young.

MORAL

A man really means business when he relies on himself rather than on his friends.

THE GUNDOG AND THE HARE

During a hunt a dog chased a hare out of a bush, and even though he was an experienced gundog, he found that the hare was streaking ahead. No matter how hard he tried, he could not catch up.

A goatherd who had been watching the hunt laughed at the dog. "How is it that a big, strong dog like you can't run as fast as an animal as small as that?" he cried.

"It's one thing," answered the dog, "to run because you want to catch something, and quite a different thing to run to save your life."

MORAL

Determination is as important as size or strength.

THE SUN AND THE WIND

The north wind and the sun got into an argument one day about who was stronger. They agreed that the best way to decide the question was to see which of them could make a man strip off his clothes.

The wind tried first. It blew fiercely, but its cold gusts only made the man pull his clothes more tightly around him. Then the wind blew even harder and the man became so cold that he put on an extra layer. Eventually the wind gave up and let the sun try.

The sun started by shining with a gentle warmth, which made the man take off his overcoat. Then it sent out hotter rays, and the man soon took off his jacket. Finally it blazed with all its strength, and the man, who could stand the heat no longer, stripped off all his clothes and went to swim in a nearby river.

MORAL

Persuasion is often more effective than force.

THE FOX AND THE CROW

A fox once saw a crow perched on the branch of a tree, holding a piece of meat in his beak. The fox, who was rather hungry, decided that he wanted the meat for himself, so he walked up to the foot of the tree and began to speak to the crow, telling him what a handsome bird he was.

"What glossy feathers you have," said the wily fox, "and what bright eyes. If your voice is as impressive as your looks, you should be the king of the birds."

The crow was flattered and, eager to prove he had a good voice, he opened his beak and croaked for all he was worth. As the fox had hoped, the piece of meat fell to the ground. The fox quickly gobbled it up and said, "If you added brains to all your other qualities, you'd make an ideal king."

MORAL

Vanity is the mark of a fool.

THE FLUTE-PLAYING WOLF

A young goat, who was dawdling along behind the rest of his herd, suddenly found himself face to face with a wolf. Before the wolf could pounce, the goat cried, "I know you're going to make a meal out of me. But before you kill me, please play the flute for a moment so that I can dance."

Thinking this could do no harm, the wolf agreed. But the music and dancing made quite a commotion, and before the song was over, a group of dogs arrived. They chased the wolf away, and the goat was able to run off after his friends.

"Serves me right," said the wolf. "I shouldn't have tried to be a flute-player when I had a hunter's work to do."

MORAL

Don't be distracted from what you set out to do.

The Marriage of the Sun

One summer's day all the animals threw a party because they heard that the sun was going to be married. The frogs were among the most boisterous in their rejoicing until an older toad hopped up and interrupted their dancing. "You fools," he said, "is this a time to celebrate? The heat from one sun is enough to dry up every pond. What do you think will happen if, after he marries, the sun has children as powerful as he is?"

MORAL

When you celebrate something, make sure it's worthwhile.

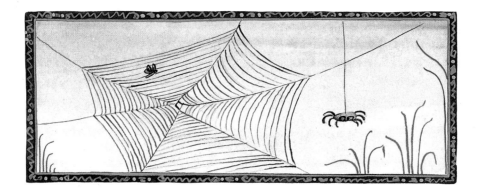

THE GNAT'S STICKY END

One day a gnat settled on a lion's ear and said to the lion, "I'm not afraid of you. I can do everything just as well as you can. You say that you can scratch with your claws and bite with your teeth, but anyone can do that, so I'm not impressed. I'm really much stronger than you, and to prove it, I'll fight you."

The gnat then latched onto the lion's face, viciously biting around his nose. The lion tore at his face to try to knock off the gnat, but his paws were too big and clumsy to find the gnat, and he did nothing but cut himself. Eventually he had to admit defeat.

The delighted gnat gave a victorious cry and flew away triumphant. But a moment later he found himself caught in a spider's web. As the owner of the web crept up to claim his meal, the gnat cried, "Oh, isn't life unfair! Here I am, fresh from defeating the strongest creature in the animal kingdom, and now I'm about to be destroyed by nothing bigger than a spider."

MORAL

Victory is often short-lived.